Where Does It Go?

PEE, RAIN, AND OTHER LIQUIDS

Written by Helen Greathead

Illustrated by Kyle Beckett

Gareth Stevens PUBLISHING

Every effort has been made by the Publishers to ensure that the websites in this book are suitable for children, that they are of the highest educational value, and that they contain no inappropriate or offensive material. However, because of the nature of the internet, it is impossible to guarantee that the contents of these sites will not be altered. We strongly advise that internet access is supervised by a responsible adult.

Please visit our website, www.garethstevens.com. For a free color catalog of all our high-quality books, call toll free 1-800-542-2595 or fax 1-877-542-2596.

Cataloging-in-Publication Data

Names: Greathead, Helen, author. | Beckett, Kyle, illustrator.
Title: Pee, rain, and other liquids / Helen Greathead, illustrated by Kyle Beckett.
Description: Buffalo, NY : Gareth Stevens Publishing, 2026. | Series: Where does it go? | Includes glossary and index.
Identifiers: ISBN 9781482475845 (pbk.) | ISBN 9781482475852 (library bound) | ISBN 9781482475869 (ebook)
Subjects: LCSH: Liquids--Juvenile literature. | Matter--Properties--Juvenile literature.
Classification: LCC QC145.24 G724 2026 | DDC 530.4'2--dc23

Published in 2026 by
Gareth Stevens Publishing
2544 Clinton St.
Buffalo, NY 14224

First published in Great Britain in 2023 by Wayland

Commissioning Editor: Elise Short
Editor: Nicola Edwards
Designers: Anthony Hannant and Gemma Steward
Science consultant: Peter Riley

Printed in China
CPSIA compliance information: Batch #QW26GS: For further information contact Gareth Stevens at 1-800-542-2595.

Find us on

CONTENTS

WHAT ARE LIQUIDS?

Liquids are things such as rain, water – and pee! In this book we'll explore the water cycle and the role liquids play in keeping our planet and its people healthy. We'll find out how rock can be liquid, and look at where liquids go when we are finished with them.

One way of figuring out whether something is a liquid is by pouring it into a different container. A liquid doesn't have a shape of its own. It changes shape to fit the new container.

Liquids can be poured because they are made up of particles that slide around.

Water is a liquid.

Particles slide around.

When a liquid cools down it can change to a solid. We call solid water ice.

Particles are tightly packed.

When a liquid heats up it can change to a gas. We call the gas water produces water vapor.

Particles move all over the place.

Water might not look like much – it's see-through and water we can drink doesn't taste like anything – but it's the most important liquid on Earth!

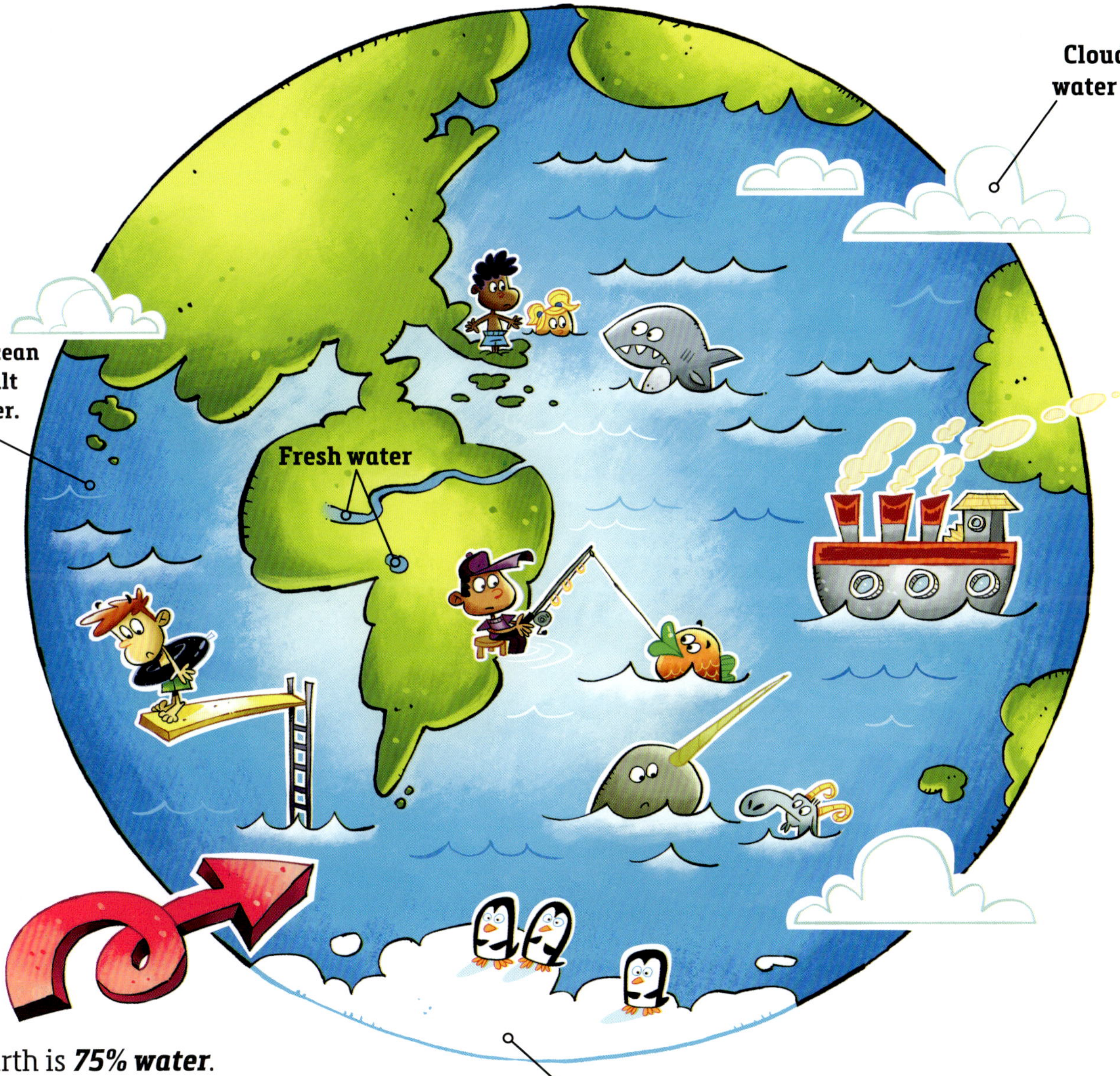

Earth is ***75% water***.
All living things need water to survive, including humans.

So let's start our journey by looking at the liquids inside you.

WATER FOR LIFE

Liquids enter your body when you drink. Most drinks contain lots of water.

You should drink ***six to eight*** glasses of water every day.

You eat water too! Some solid foods are nearly all water.

A human body can survive ***2 months*** without food! It can only survive ***2 to 4 days*** without water. A lack of water can make you thirsty, dizzy, confused, and headachy.

What's liquid and what's snot

Your body is about 60% liquid. Here are just five of the liquids that keep it working:

1. Tears, three things they can do:

1. Keep eyes clean.
2. Protect eyes, from onions that release gas when chopped, for example!
3. Flow when you're sad.

2. Saliva helps with tasting, digesting and talking. Up to 0.5 gallon (2 l) of saliva are produced each day.

3. Blood travels around your body in veins, arteries, and capillaries. It feeds oxygen and nutrients to all the body's cells. The average human body contains 1 to 1.5 gallons (4.5 to 5.5 l) of blood.

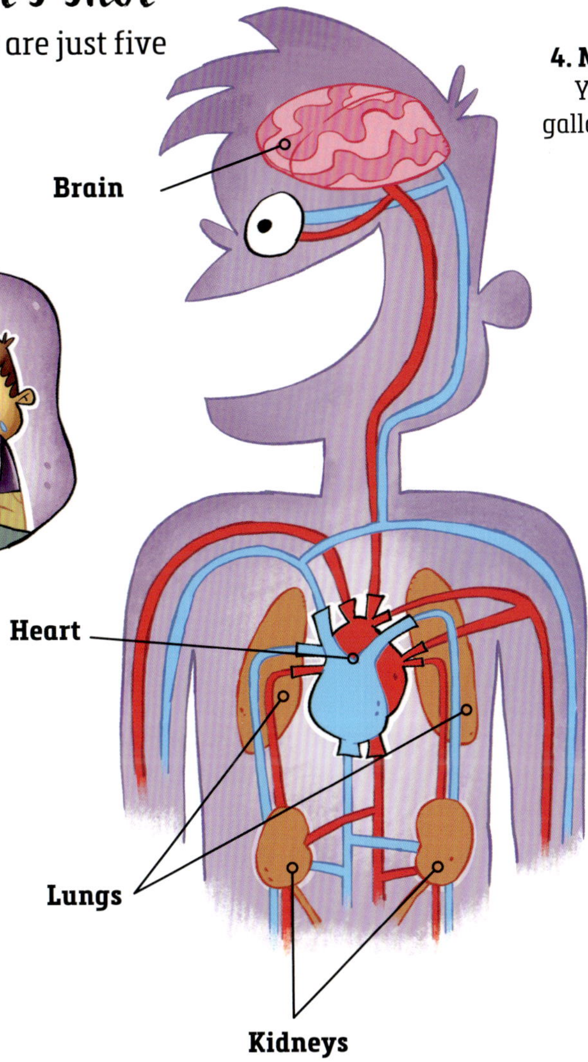

4. Mucus lines your nostrils. Your nose produces 0.25 gallon (1 l) of mucus each day.

Mucus comes out of your nose as snot!

5. Sweat is released from 2.6 million sweat glands to keep you cool.

Water is the main ingredient in all these fluids. It also carries waste from your body when you pee.

WHY WE PEE

Your body needs LOTS of water to work properly, but where does it all go? And how does it come out again?

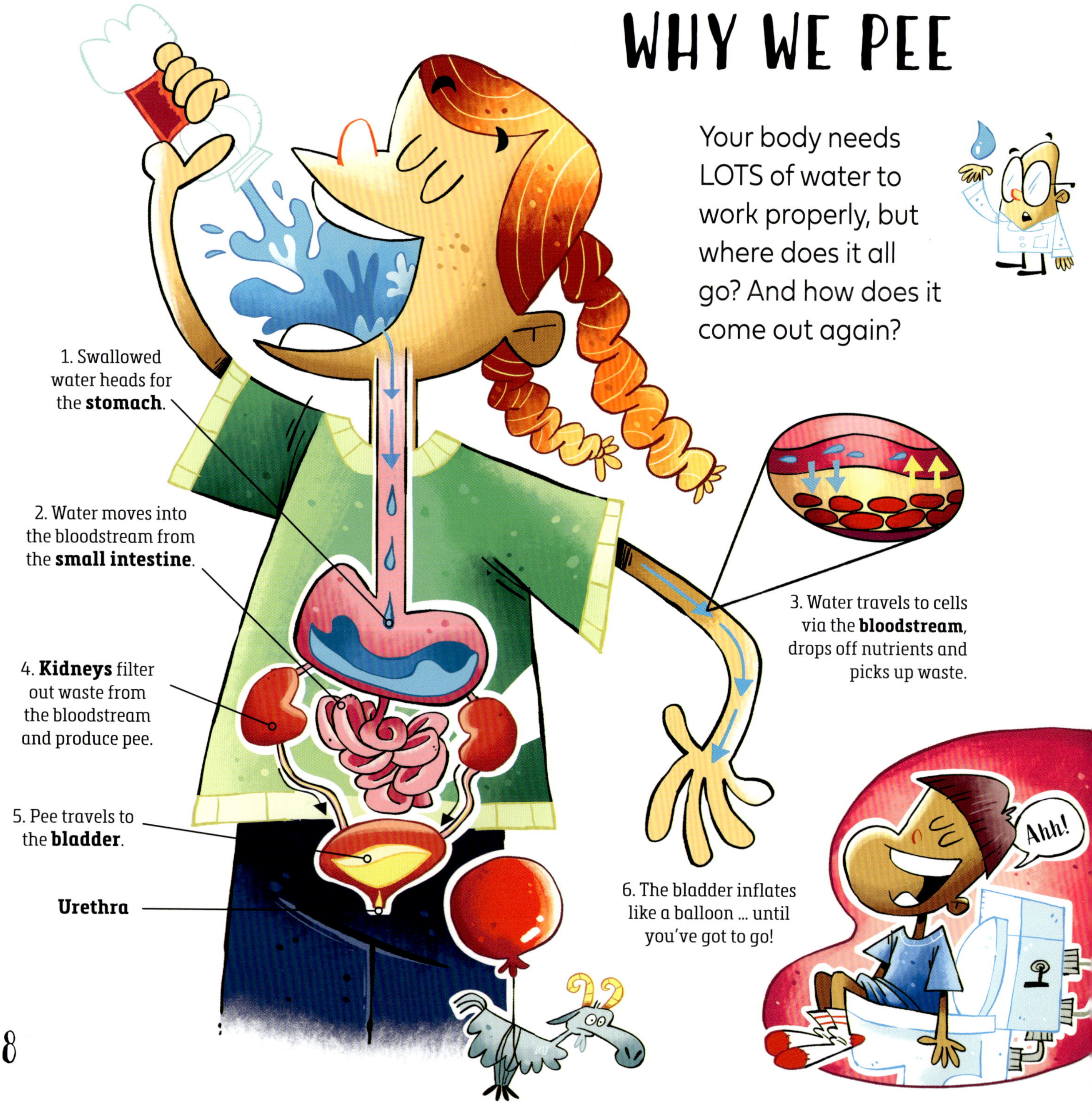

Peeing is your body's way of getting rid of poisons. It's still 95% water. The other 5% contains over ***3,000*** different chemicals, including urea – nitrogen waste that comes from proteins in your blood.

What's in your pee?

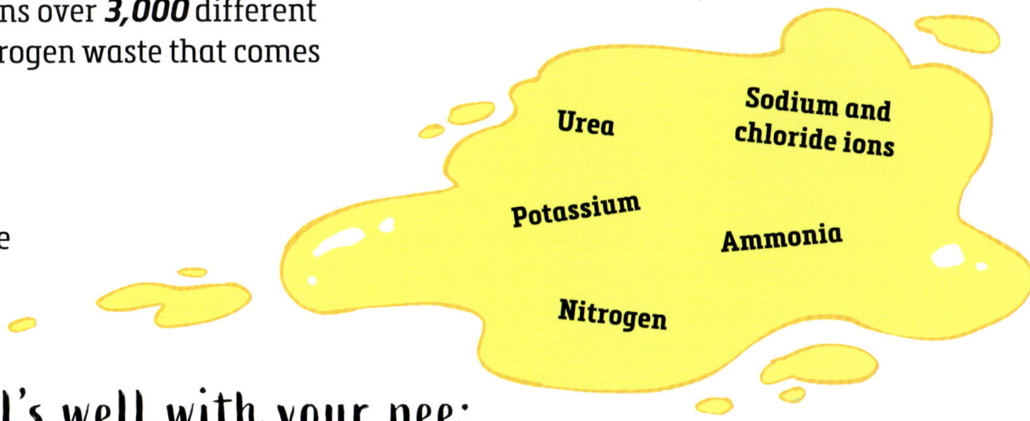

A healthy person produces ***10 fluid ounces (30 ml)*** of pee per hour.

Here's how to tell all's well with your pee:

- You pee five to seven times a day.
- It doesn't smell – unless you haven't peed for a long while, you've eaten asparagus, had a curry, or drunk coffee!
- It's almost colorless.

Find the color of your pee on the Pee Well Chart:

And flush! ...
But where does all the water in your toilet come from?

WATER ON TAP

In some houses, water appears like magic when you flush the toilet or turn on a tap. It's traveled a long way, though!

How water works:

1. Water vapor in the atmosphere cools into water droplets.
2. Droplets join together as clouds.
3. Clouds grow heavier. Droplets fall as rain.

This massive dam wall holds and stores a huge amount of water.

Some rain forms springs that trickle downhill. Springs grow into streams. Streams feed into a river.

Some rain becomes groundwater.

Some water from dams travels along pipes to a treatment plant, where it is:

1. Screened – to remove leaves, sticks, and other solids.

2. Clarified – with chemicals that make dirt particles stick together and easier to remove.

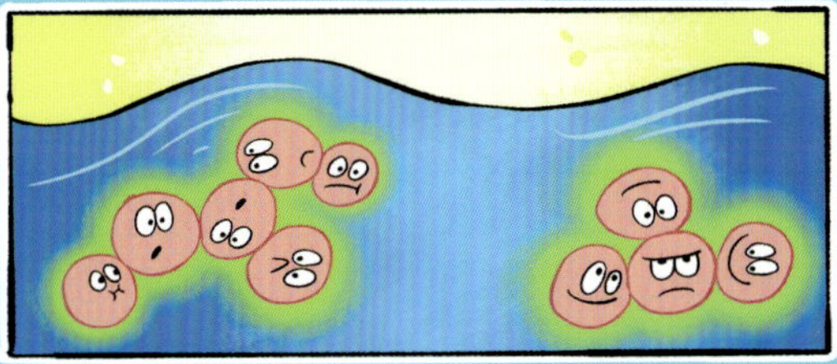

3. Filtered – through sand and gravel.

4. Disinfected – with chemicals that kill off anything that could cause infection.

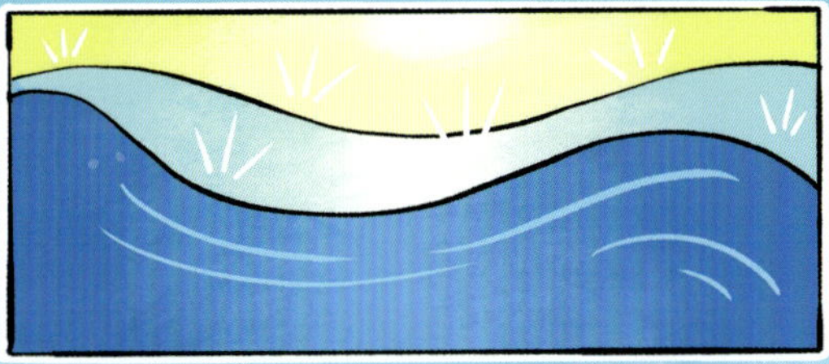

In a home with a water supply, one person can use ***155 gallons (590 l)*** of water in a day.

A person without access to a water supply might use only ***3 gallons (11 l)*** of water a day.

5. Sparkling clean water is pumped along miles of pipeline to your home. Turning on a tap releases pressure, so water can flow out.

6. Then, when your pee is flushed away, it mixes with other waste household liquids.

So what might those other liquids be?

KETCHUP AND MORE

The liquids in your home don't all behave like water ...

2. Oils come from pressed seeds, fruits, nuts, or animal fat. Unlike water, they have color and flavor. They can be liquid or solid:

1. Ketchup is called a "soft solid." It can only move like a liquid with help.

Shaking mixes solid tomato particles with water particles, until ketchup flows.

Oil and water are so different, they don't mix.

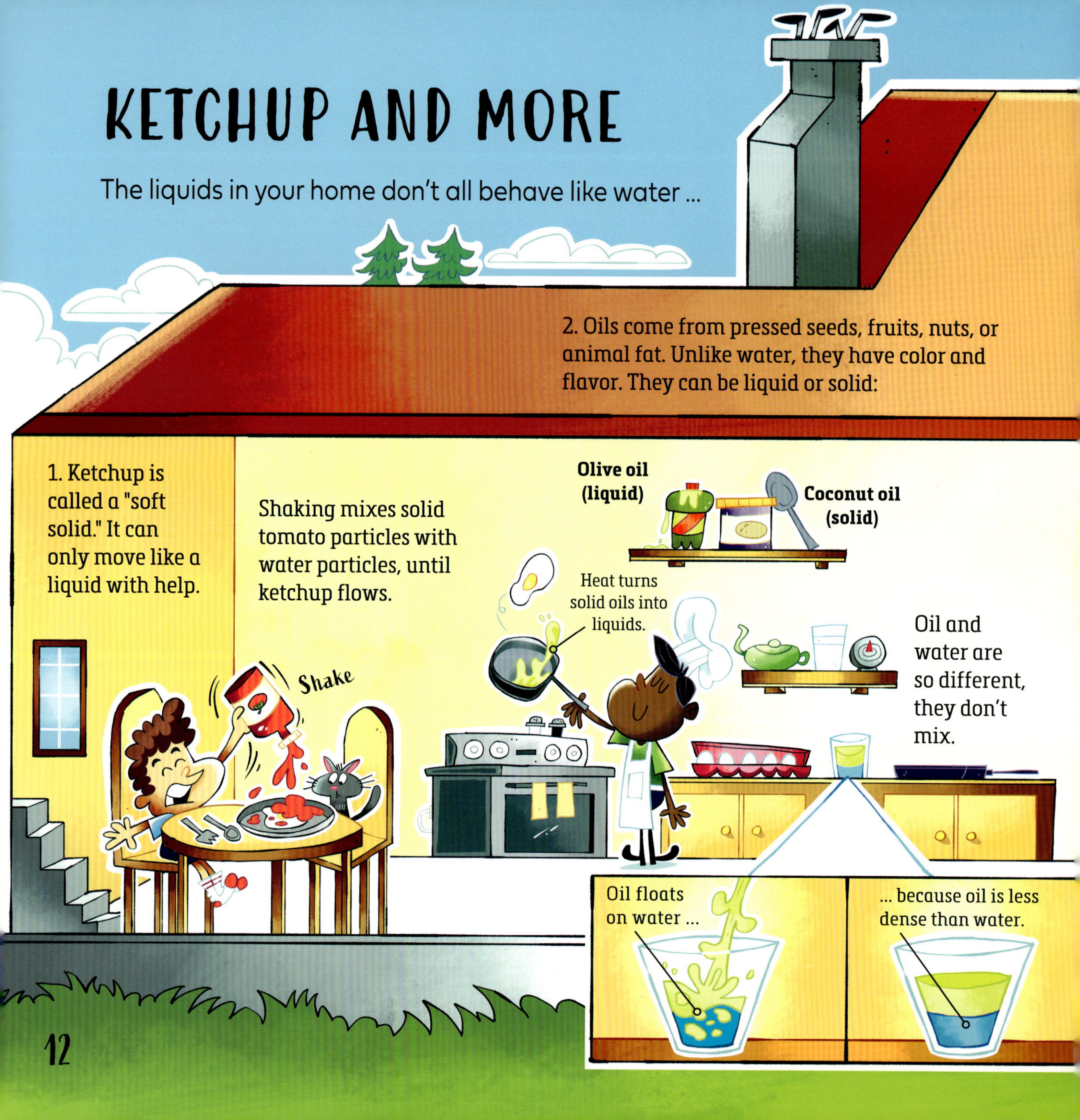

3. Molecules of liquid dish soap look a bit like tadpoles.

Soapy molecules in the sink surround blobs of oil (and dirt). To escape the water, the molecule tails worm their way into the oil, breaking it apart.

4. Heat from a candle flame melts the wax.

Tightly packed particles in the solid candle spread out in the melted wax.

Wax becomes solid when cool.

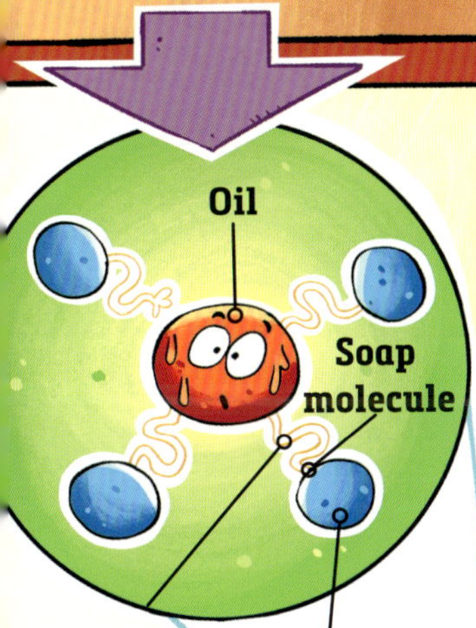

5. Once they're finished, these liquids can go down the drain with the dirty, soapy dishwater:

These liquids can't:

But what happens when the wrong liquids disappear down the drain?

A MATTER OF FAT

Wastewater from inside and outside your home travels down underground pipes to the sewer system. It joins wastewater from other houses.

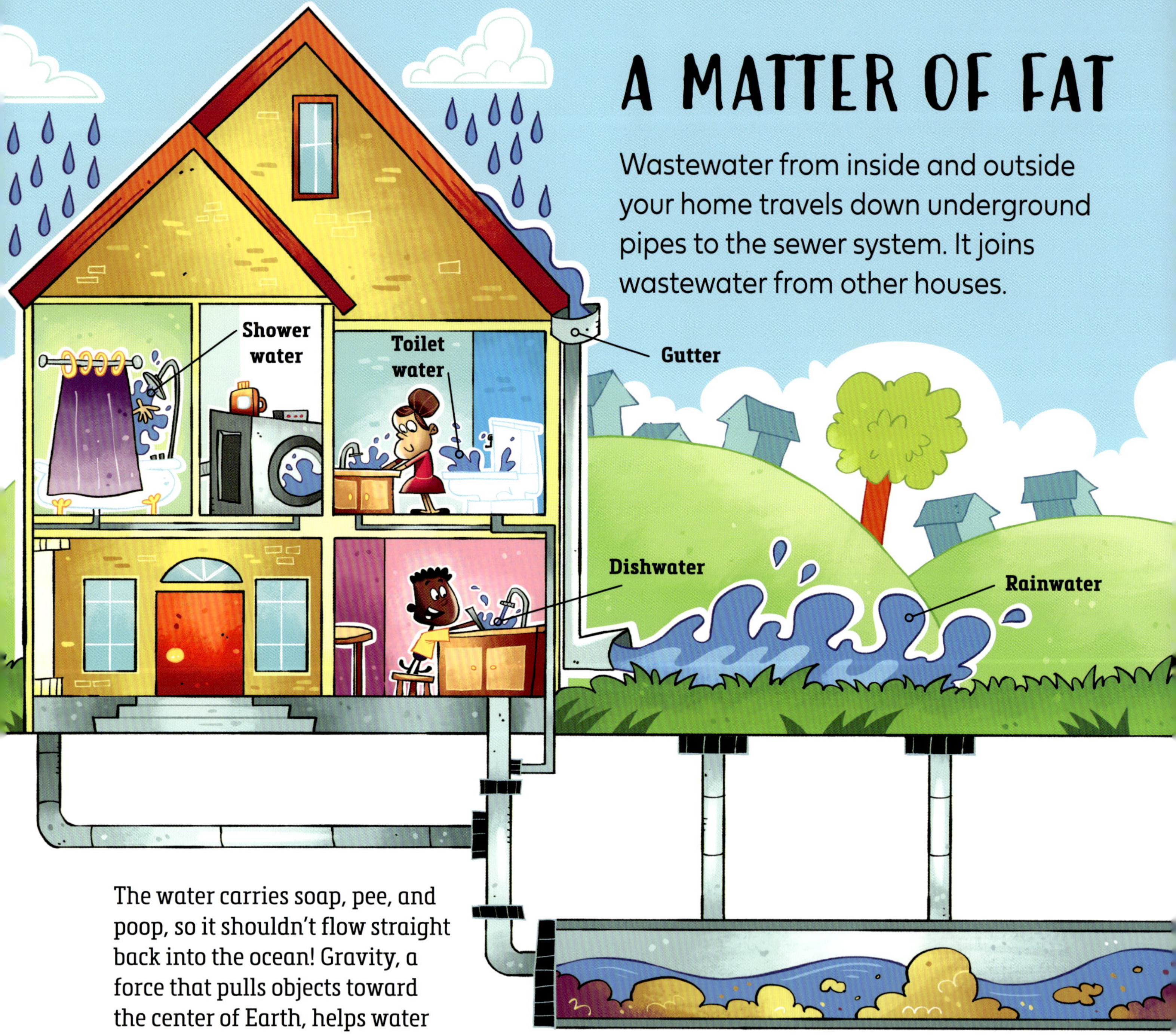

The water carries soap, pee, and poop, so it shouldn't flow straight back into the ocean! Gravity, a force that pulls objects toward the center of Earth, helps water to swoosh down pipes toward a treatment center ...

But sometimes unwanted waste blocks the pipes!

Festering fatbergs

Liquid oils and fats cool into solids in the sewer pipes.

In 2021, a fatberg the weight of **250 family cars** blocked drains in Birmingham, UK.

1

Lumps of solid fat ...

2

... are joined by wet wipes.

3

More fat, poop, baby wipes, diapers, and cotton swabs arrive. Dangerous bacteria cling on.

4

The lump grows into a huge solid, called a fatberg!

It cost nearly ***$30,000*** to remove one smallish fatberg in South West Australia.

When fatbergs block drains, pipes can burst. Pee, poop, and more could come back out!

If we were more careful about what we sent down the drain, fatbergs wouldn't exist! The oil could still be recycled.

The blockage has been cleared – phew! Now that it can flow, where does that dirty water go?

WHAT HAPPENS TO PEE?

When your wastewater reaches a water treatment plant (see page 11), it pours into settlement tanks.

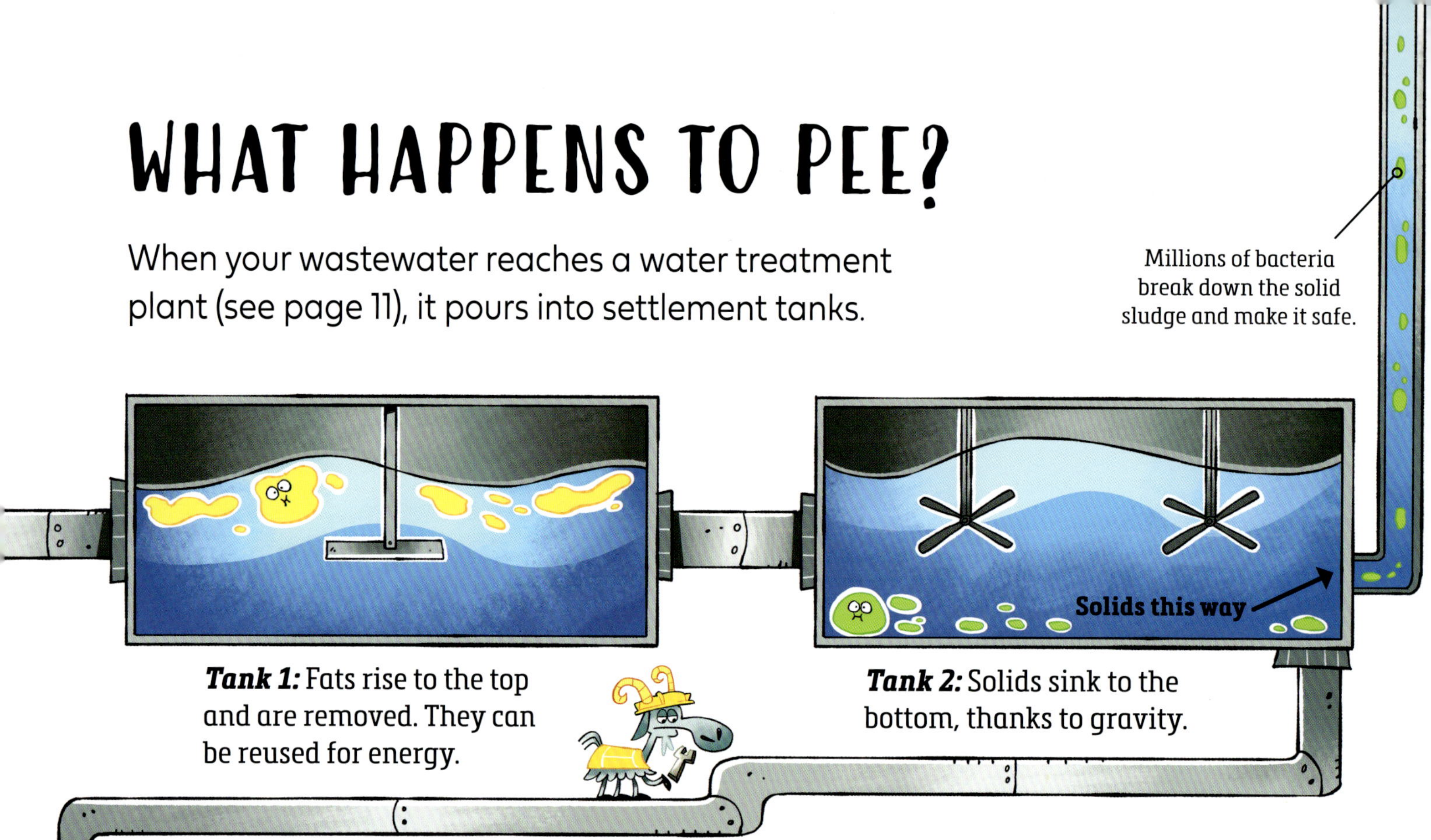

Tank 1: Fats rise to the top and are removed. They can be reused for energy.

Tank 2: Solids sink to the bottom, thanks to gravity.

Tank 3: Bubbles of air pump through the water to remove smells. Chemicals remove nutrients that could cause unwanted plant growth. The water is now easier to filter.

Tank 4: In the filtration tank there are layers of sand and small pebbles. These layers trap the fine dirt. Some newer water treatment plants no longer need this tank.

Tank 5: Water is tested to make sure it is clean and safe to be released into a river or the ocean, and back into the water cycle (see page 20).

After testing, the water might also flow back to your home!

Historical pee

Hundreds of years ago, the Romans had some interesting uses for pee ...

Recommended to soothe scorpion stings.

Romans could sell their pee! It was:

And collected on street corners. Urea (see page 9) releases ammonia that gets stains out of clothes!

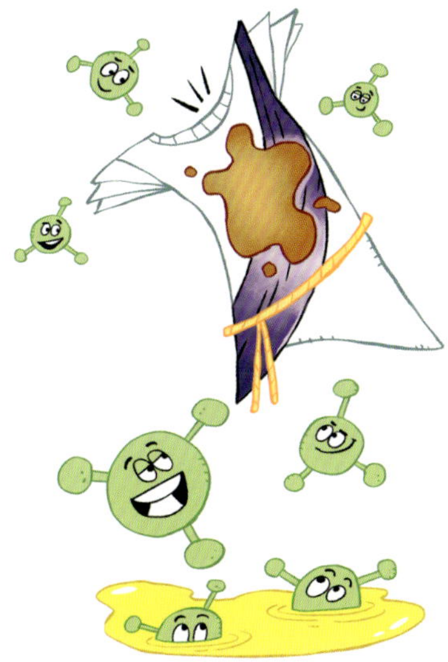

Today in some rich and poor countries, dirty wastewater runs into rivers and seas, damaging wildlife.

Does pee harm the sea?

PEE IN THE SEA

Did you know that 2.2 million animals species live – and pee – in the ocean? Their pee can be really useful.

Minerals in a sea creature's pee help sea life grow!

1. Whale pee and sunlight makes plankton (food for fish) grow.

2. Krill eat plankton.

Krill

3. Other creatures eat krill.

A fin whale can pee **255 gallons (970 l)** in one

The pee from larger sea animals contains extra phosphorus from the bones of the creatures they eat. It helps corals to grow 1.5 times faster. When humans catch too many of these larger creatures for food, they put other sea life in danger.

Too much pee

Sometimes, large amounts of human wastewater overflow into the sea. When wastewater mixes with chemical fertilizer run off, strange things can happen.

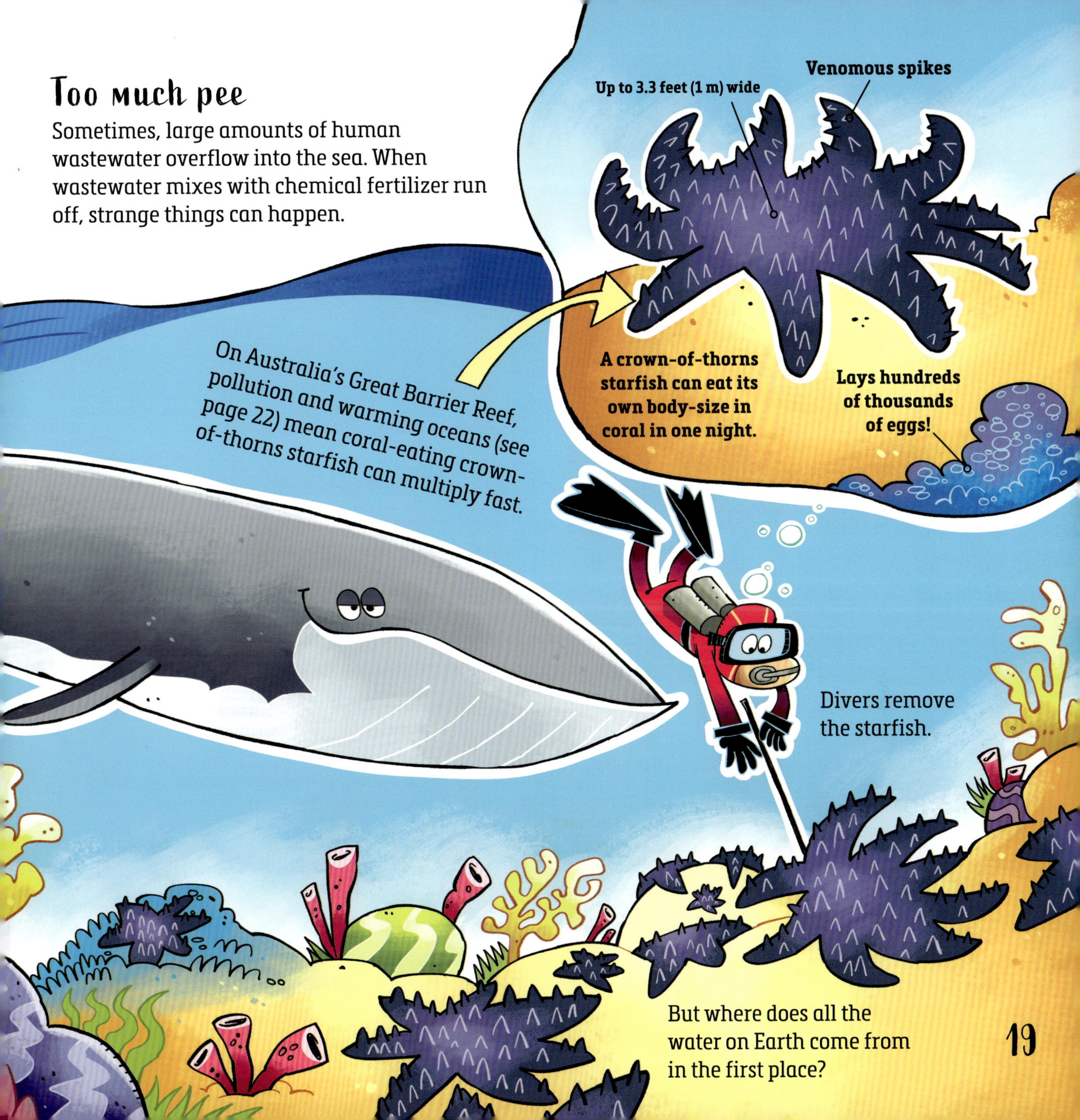

On Australia's Great Barrier Reef, pollution and warming oceans (see page 22) mean coral-eating crown-of-thorns starfish can multiply fast.

Divers remove the starfish.

But where does all the water on Earth come from in the first place?

IT'S RAINING DINOSAUR PEE

Incredibly, Earth has had the same amount of water ever since it formed. That water has been changing from liquid to solid to gas for billions of years! Here's how:

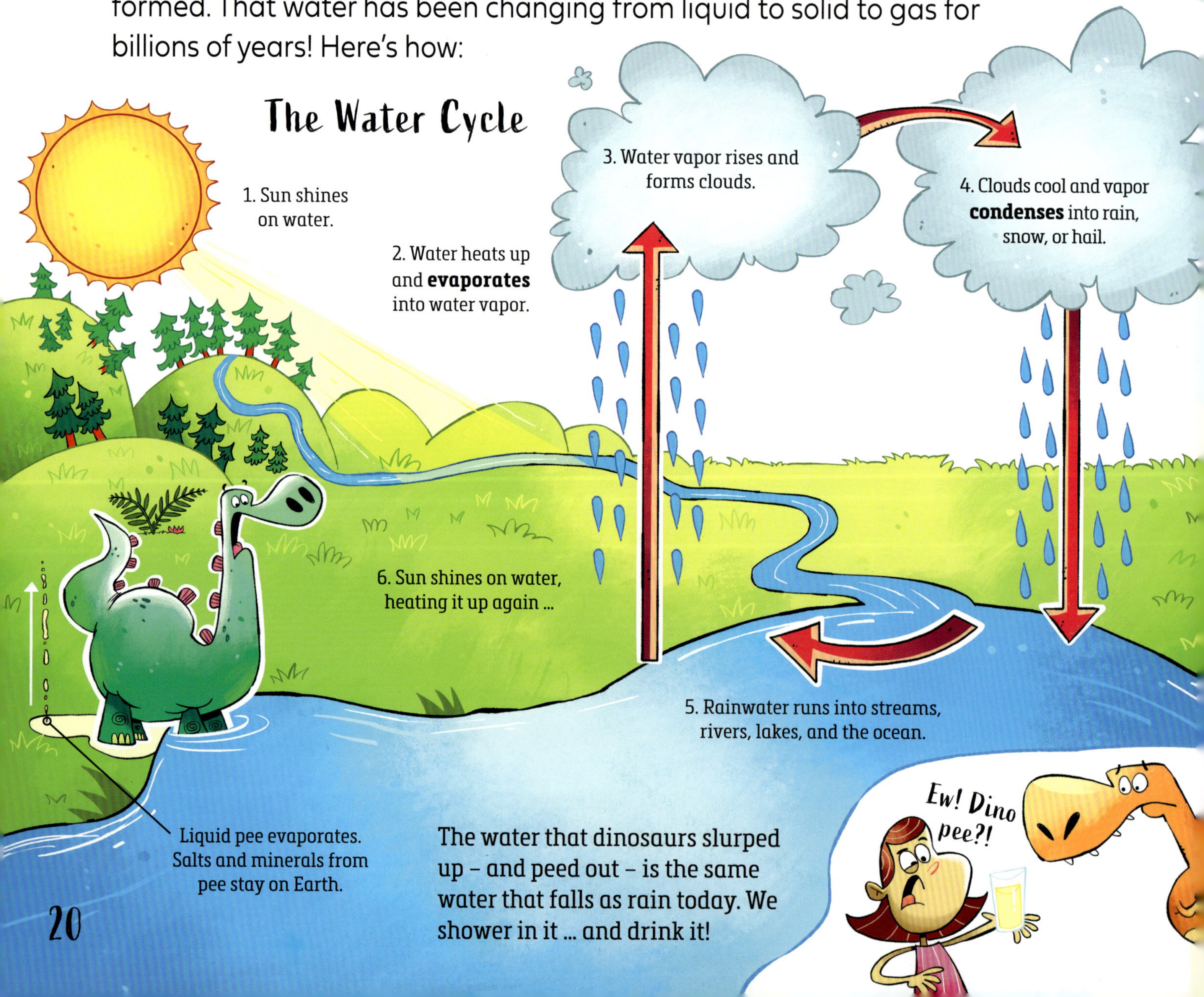

The water that dinosaurs slurped up – and peed out – is the same water that falls as rain today. We shower in it ... and drink it!

Wet, wet, wet

Mawsynram, India, is one of the world's wettest places. In June 2022, over ***3.3 feet (1 m)*** of rain fell in just ***24 hours***.

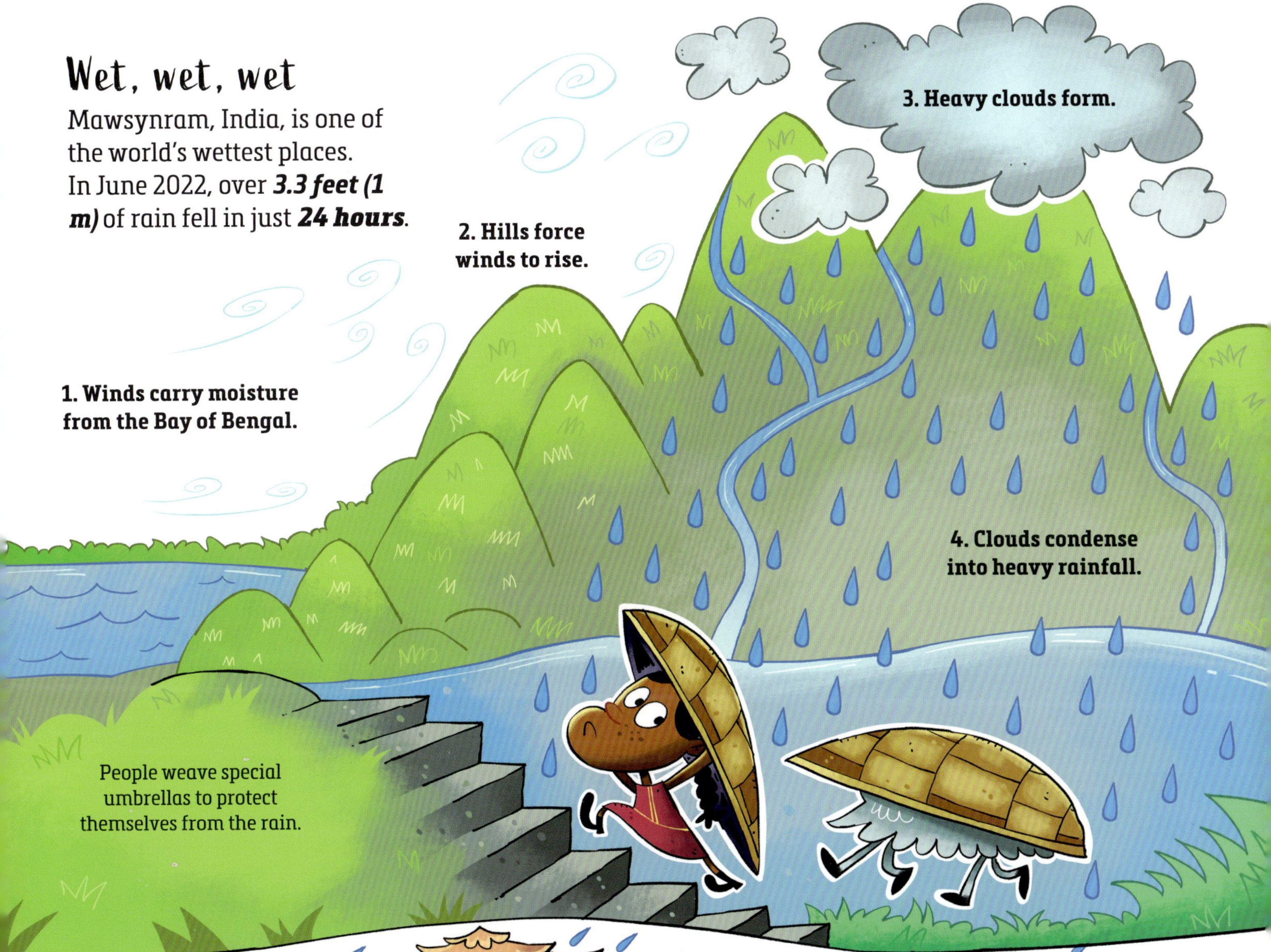

Local children have rain holidays when it's too wet to get to school.

Parts of the world are getting wetter. How can we cope with too much water?

SOAK IT UP

Human activities, such as driving gas-powered cars and farming animals for food, produce too much carbon dioxide (CO_2) and methane gases. These extra gases trap sunlight, making Earth and the ocean warmer.

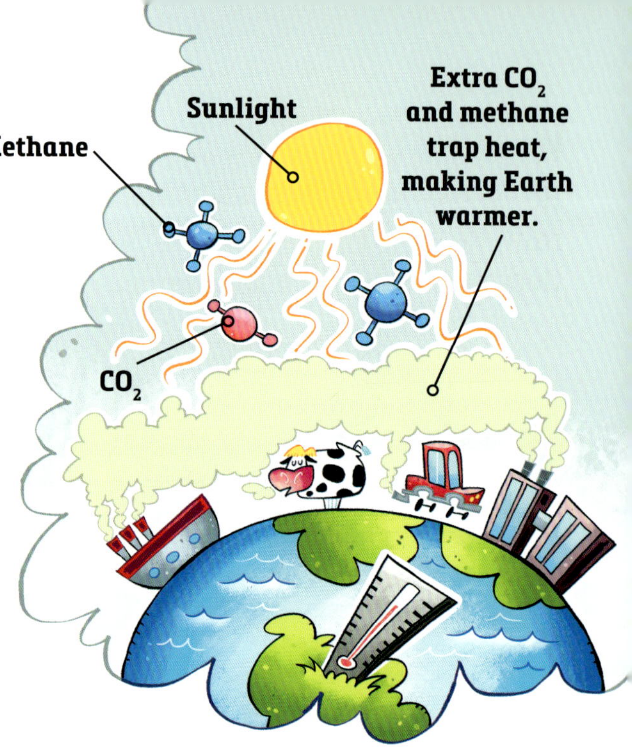

Warmer air carries more water vapor, bringing fast, heavy rains. When city drains can't cope with rainwater, it starts to collect and floods happen.

6 inches (15 cm) of fast-flowing floodwater is enough to knock a person off their feet.

Floodwater ruins crops, pollutes drinking water, carries disease, and causes billions of dollars' worth of damage.

Welcome to Sponge City

Heavy rains hit some Chinese cities during the rainy season. Concrete roads and buildings leave floodwater with nowhere to go.

But one Chinese designer has a solution – he's designing cities that soak up rainwater like a sponge, and reuse it.

Rain and concrete roads don't mix well.

China plans to have ***30*** sponge cities by 2030. It will cost over ***$1 trillion*** to build them!

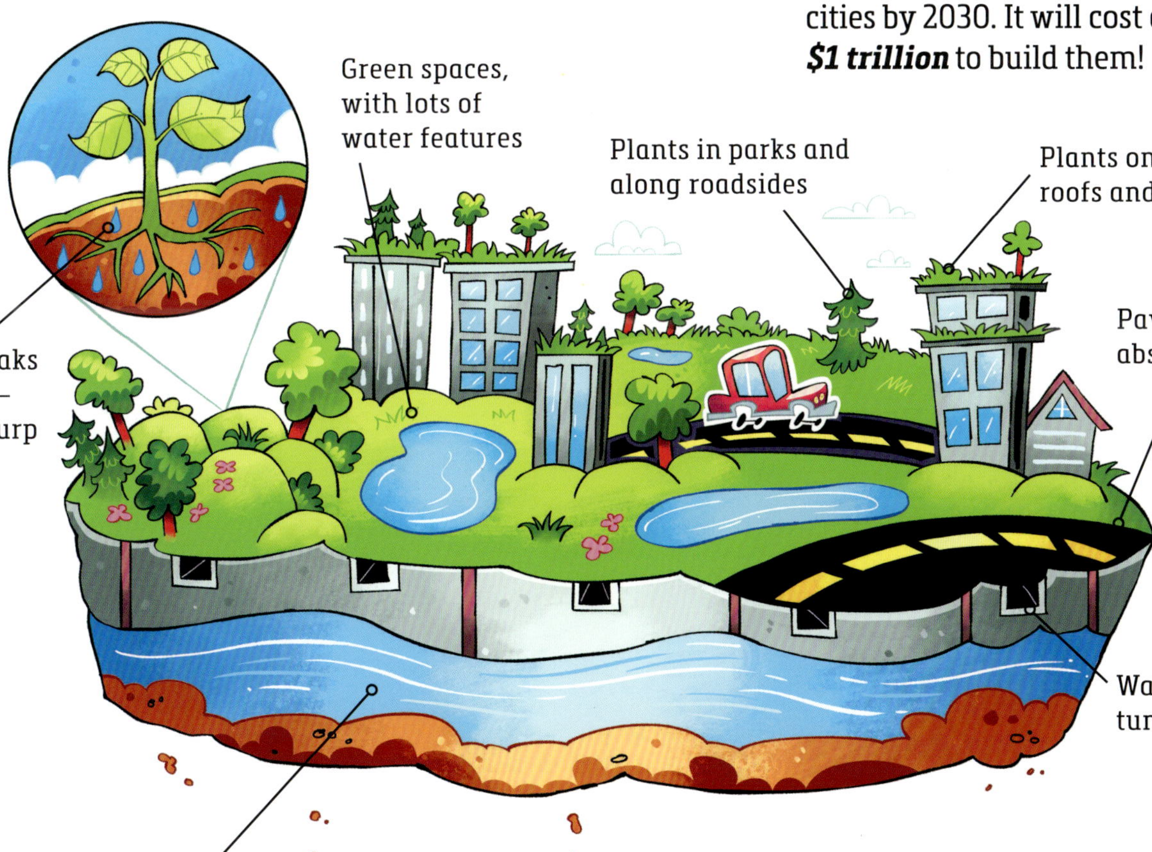

Meanwhile, some places have trouble getting all the water they need ...

WATER, WATER, EVERYWHERE

By 2030, the United Nations has pledged that everyone in the world should have access to safe water. But can that happen where rain hardly falls?

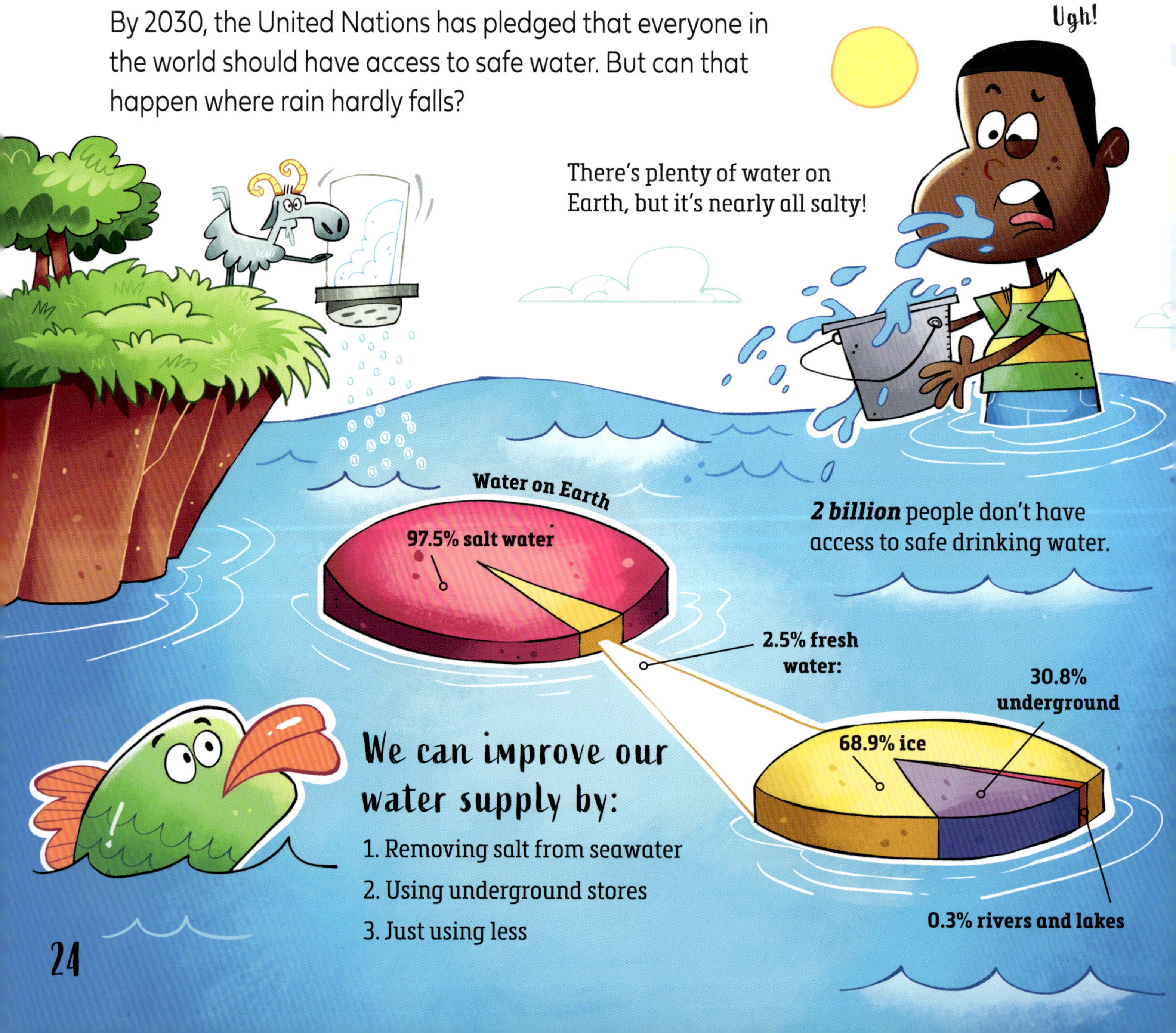

2 billion people don't have access to safe drinking water.

We can improve our water supply by:

1. Removing salt from seawater
2. Using underground stores
3. Just using less

Some parts of the world are getting drier. As world temperatures increase (see page 22), water evaporates faster from rivers, oceans, and soil.

There's more water vapor in the atmosphere but less liquid water on land – and rain falls unevenly.

And then there's ...

... Fog-catching

It hardly ever rains in Lima, Peru, so water usually comes from melting ice on nearby mountain peaks, or glaciers. As temperatures rise, the glaciers are shrinking. But there's a plan to capture moisture from fog hanging over the city!

In the future, these tall towers could provide ***950,000 gallons (3.6 million l)*** of water a year for Lima.

But it's not just water that causes problems. Other liquids can also bring disaster.

LIQUID LAND

Even earth and solid rock can become liquid!

Shaking all over

An earthquake hit Christchurch, New Zealand, in 2011, that shook the ground and turned it to jelly. Buildings collapsed – including some that were earthquake-proofed!

Scientists call this liquefaction. It doesn't happen often. Today, in New Zealand, new structures get really strong foundations and builders check the ground before they build.

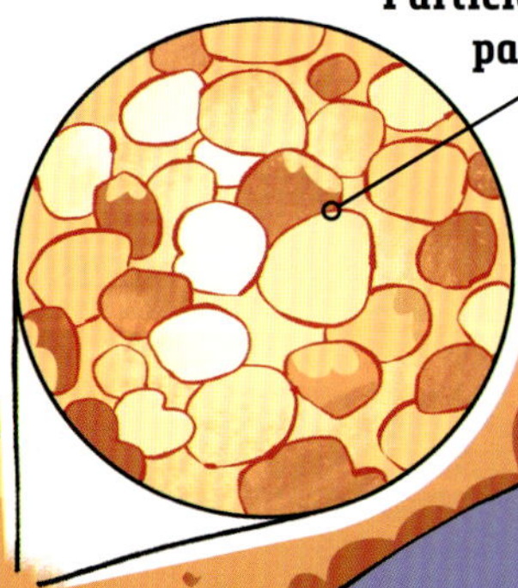

Hot rock

Earth may look solid, but there's scorching hot liquid in its middle:

When a volcano erupts, magma whooshes through holes in Earth's crust. It mixes with gases, flowing out as lava.

Lava flows at a speed of ***a few feet per hour***.

There's usually time to run away.

The fastest lava flow ever was ***37 miles (60 km) per hour*** in the Democratic Republic of the Congo in 1977.

Lava destroys everything in its path ... but it can cool to form brand new islands. Surtsey, near Iceland, appeared after undersea eruptions in the 1960s.

Liquids created many of Earth's features too.

THE POWER OF WATER

Water is always moving. Streams and rivers flow downhill, pulled by gravity, until they rush into the ocean. As it flows, water smooths rock edges, moves trees and other plants and carries away pieces of rock and dirt. This is called erosion.

Over thousands of years, rivers can carve rock into deep valleys or giant waterfalls.

Because of the power of water, the landscape is always changing shape. Niagara Falls in Ontario, Canada, is eroding at a rate of ***1 foot (300 mm)*** a year. In ***50,000 years*** it will have disappeared!

Liquids are at the center of our world. They are essential to all life on Earth and even help to make it beautiful!

As Earth warms, the balance of ice, water vapor, and liquid water will change, but the water cycle will stay the same (see page 20). So there will always be just as much water on our planet – in liquid, gas, or solid form – as there was millions of years ago, when the dinosaurs peed here.

GLOSSARY

absorb – soak up

bacteria – simple, living cells that are too small to see. They can multiply fast and some can cause infection.

bloodstream – the blood that circulates around a human's or other animal's body

erode – when land is slowly worn away because of erosion, e.g. when seawater washes over rock

evaporate – when a liquid turns into a gas

fertilizer – substance that is spread on crops to help them grow

glacier – a huge, slow-moving body of ice that forms on land, e.g. a mountain top

gravity – a force that makes things fall to the ground

groundwater – water that trickles underground and is stored there

mineral – a substance that forms naturally, e.g. salt. Some minerals help to keep a human or other animal body healthy.

molecule – the smallest unit of a chemical mixture, such as water

nitrogen – an essential nutrient for all plants

nutrient – something that feeds living things and helps them grow

particle – a tiny piece of matter

phosphorus – a substance that is essential to all living things. In humans and other animals it is important for building teeth and bones.

protein – large molecules that are needed to make cells in the body

sewer system – the pipes, pumps, tanks etc., that are needed to collect and treat water

species – animals and plants that share features. Members of a species can breed (have babies) with each other.

thaw – melt

United Nations (UN) – an international organisation – with 193 member countries – that aims to keep peace around the world

water pressure – the amount of force needed to push water along a pipe

water vapor – water in the form of gas, e.g. after it has evaporated in the heat of the sun

FURTHER INFORMATION

Books

Comic Strip Science: Chemistry by Paul Mason (Wayland, 2023)

The Wee that Animals Pee by Paul Mason (Gareth Stevens Publishing, 2026)

Websites

More fatberg facts and pictures:
www.bbc.co.uk/newsround/47117422

Lots of information on the water cycle:
climatekids.nasa.gov/water-cycle

INDEX